THE BETTER MONSTERS

THE BETTER MONSTERS

PUNEET DUTT

Mansfield Press

Printed in Canada

Library and Archives Canada Cataloguing in Publication

Dutt, Puneet, author
The better monsters / Puneet Dutt.

Poems.
ISBN 978-1-77126-156-2 (softcover)

I. Title.

PS8607.U89B48 2017 C811'.6 C2017-906386-3

Typesetting & Cover Design: Denis De Klerck

The publication of *The Better Monsters* has been generously supported by the Canada Council for the Arts and the Ontario Arts Council.

ONTARIO ARTS COUNCIL
CONSEIL DES ARTS DE L'ONTARIO
an Ontario government agency
un organisme du gouvernement de l'Ontario

Canada Council for the Arts
Conseil des arts du Canada

Mansfield Press Inc.
25 Mansfield Avenue, Toronto, Ontario, Canada M6J 2A9
Publisher: Denis De Klerck
www.mansfieldpress.net

To Gaurav—always

TABLE OF CONTENTS

"...outsiders whose language and customs I do not understand, so foreign that in extreme instances I am reluctant to admit they belong to the same species as my own."

—Tzvetan Todorov

"This identity-bit, in the most colloquial sense, can only be described through the political affect of the Green (no longer phenomenally so) or Alien Registration (Identity) Card. An unnameable identity, named only as "alien," yet strong enough, again, for public self-identification with the protesters in the nation."

—Gayatri Chakravorty Spivak

SPEAK AMERICAN

grew up watching
westerns   cowboys
Elmer Fudd Looney Tunes
laughed at the puff of smoke
behind the chase
rooted the holder
dreamt water pistols
shot down the boy
behind the tree
sought paintball nights
in university
a splatter of blue bruises
source of pride
how to then shed this skin
wrapped since youth
how to speak American
when we arrive
without our imagination
to bring down bodies
have we lived American until
we've held the clip of a
Nerf gun
dreamt in shots
paid for the fantasy of elimination
in movie theatres

have you seen that film?

OVER CIDER AND WHISKEY IN HOTEL ROOMS

I.

the food was terrible
at Gitmo

there was a pub that made nasty things
except for
jerk chicken

they had a Jamaican chef
in Cuba

II.

his experience was totally different
from mine

i only saw Kabul

school girls in blue uniform
burqas

air so dirty
they burned their
plastics

anything

goat bones and garbage
got in the lungs

a health disclaimer
to those who stay
long enough

III.

i wore a lapis blue burqa
walked the streets
sweat from head to toe

some colors
pale yellow pastel
could be worn

palaw
like when saffron
apricot peels
sizzle in one pan

even then
you never really see much

IV.

never saw Jalalabad
though i was there

the great fear was
pedestrians
IEDs latched
on to moving cars

in Kabul
the city pulses
                practically throbs
crowds surge
at every corner
they eye zinc baths and apples
on Chicken Street

we'd be so annoyed
when someone would slap the car
to pass and cross

we'd all have to get out
   and check

V.

did you ever,
          i mean—
    kill someone?

VI.

it was different the first tour
i knew no one

there was lots of money then
lots

in Fallujah
they would bring in Filipino chefs
we'd have
barbecues

salsa instructors flown in
from Miami
Olympic coaches
for 5ks
full marathons
inside the compound

the second?
i was lucky
i made a friend

men went batshit

fought themselves
    kept from doing stupid things

shooting a toe

            or worse

VII.

we became aware of certain
    'norms'
for some
in southern Afghanistan

small villages
jammed the foot
of mountains

in bombing campaigns
farmers would say

    compensate us
    you've killed my goats

otherwise
they were lucky if they owned
a craft shop
on the base   rugs and such

                                        i don't know
                              to see fighters
from another country with guns
in my local market everyday
not knowing what they were doing
i would hate them

    exactly

VIII.

boys
little boys
   just eight or 12 most

sold through the Taliban

families can't afford
to keep

what happens after 12

they're let go

what happens to them after

more boys
more men
dress boys up
as women

paint their faces
make them dance with bells for

whole villages
know this

IX.

one man who'd been fucking goats so long
came in to ask
why his wife wasn't getting
pregnant

he'd been in her ass for months
each day
sometimes
            twice a day

X.

can't say i ever killed a man
but can't say
i didn't

                you?

can't say

i controlled the web
so i bargained with that

in some ways
i was God to them

                you?

i was eyes
watching from above

    so in some ways

XI.

and now you're back
    what's next?

XII.

haven't _______
for a year

finally agreed

another job
far away
is an option

gives us space

time

he doesn't admit he's we've just bought a
Cape Cod dusk blue we talk about where we'll
plant tomato seeds and there's rabbits deer and
foxes that come our neighbors are directors at
CNN interior designers cool jobs and we're
like the losers coming back cuz there's still this
America where
what we did is held in disdain we can't talk
about what we did how sometimes it's different
from the way it's *shown* but they think they know
and we can't tell them we can't even tell each
other not really not all of it a whole other life
no wonder we can't admit
we would lose our clearance but then if we
don't we'll lose

XIII.

some nights we slept to the sound of shelling and explosions
          like nothing

one was so strong
i was thrown from bed

got up
and went back to sleep

XIV.

then you get back

just a week
between rest   and a desk

computer screen
suit

fixed jobs for those
who return

all limbed
no meds

"Who are you people be? If you are coming-in people be, then come in."

—Gabriel Okara

JC MAY

on long Saturdays
between the work week
and day of rest
dreams are narrow

BHAARAT MOONSHINE

you
you do not know what it is to drink six last names three
countries and singh kaur dutt dutta datt datta and howl
at the moon
you stand bold at our liquid bends exotica without final
fathers begging bowls since Partition
itch at an Englishman's mirage
parched for history
who took whom
married whom
who hooked who on what tree
these kinked marks sound something of cave in me
i do not know what quivers
our blue gods of butter that beat reed brooms ask gifts
of goats and call it 'culture'
tikhi's at *Chandni Chowk*
bhaarat moonshine in *dhotis*
dead presidents and queens greening on iron coins of
Sanskrit
the weight of silver bullets lodged in our lungs
that grandmother smuggled
this idea of India still running on loop
how far from
far
are we?

THE BETTER MONSTERS

we didn't have
the better monsters:

white vans rattling

taped cardboard
windows

drinks in
brown paper bags

beneath the full sun
from one street to another
cross skipping rope
at Pershing Field
children disappear

hopscotch chalk
smudged
behind

BEHIND THE REGISTER

  99 cents for 4

you must be 21 and over
to buy
tomato seeds
  beet
  celery
  cucumber

packets line the walls of
the Farmers' Market
in neat rows on Kennedy Ave.
beside the San André factory
my sister calls *the sweatshop*
secured behind the register
because kids are smoking them

ALIEN ALIEN

"he pays cash, that's why he's called Mister."
—Oswald Joseph Mtshali

never had an education
took a *talvar* to school
and fled the country

records of Saturday Night Fevers
bell bottom stone-washed jeans
played his youth

eyes closed
he reached Queens

doors closed to his
dark room body
doors always closed
no matter the knock
we were toes and whispers
children of his parent's eyes

he left his records behind
wallet open to VHS's
CDs
Deep Purple Aerosmith Bon Jovi
another hit

long drives
alone in a white U-Haul
and all the trucks he ever haggled for
that broke down from so many miles

Hey God, I'm just a little man got a wife and family
he knew the songs
the CK jeans

Yankee's cap
they sold him

her and him
two suitcases each
so fast they left us
to get there

Memphis to New Orleans
i asked him
her
what did you see
criss-crossed veins
America
alligators and beads
the giant peach
what did you see

dekhna kyah tah
what was there

we'd long for postcards
textbooks
Mount Rushmore Gettysburg America
highways
highways
5 a.m. and stand
fleamarkets sun under tarp
until now they can't stand anymore

i find them again
on the same street
weary of motels and rest stops
bruised soap souvenirs
of where they've been
back to where they started
97 to 95

from Georgia and back
all along the coast
boxes we'd help make
thought it was a game
hide and seek
perfumes scrunchies barrettes
whatever they could buy

whatever they could sell
always afraid of who was at the door

she kept chipped bottles
Testers without caps
fingered blue RL America
gifted us Caution: Flammable
and sprayed
stars and stripes

we got through school this way
not being *stinky Pakis*
go home
we bought
like good greencards
when they asked
we bought
swore allegiance
to clothes and movies
credit card after credit card
found a way to stay

that English
fly tape ensnares flies with appealing colors
Made in USA
so much about
explorers
Manifest Destiny
Christopher Columbus

that America
and when they try to make rent
next month   we have it next month
we scattered
kids and weddings
north and south
they still ask us where
we're really from

implies place
when i slip a hundred in her purse
even when i dye my hair blonde
my tongue lashed by ESL
i can only interpret
a weekend
so many of us
learned
the odds are bet against us
            we alien alien

WILD STATE

"...understand yourself as rendered hypervisible in the face of such language acts."
—Claudia Rankine

when you lasso voice
down from a country
rope
burns the flesh
mother or the grandfather
die
  dirty words
  hang with friends
  in backseats
when it
forks at school where the teacher
sits on the same word
the same word
say it say it
repeat after me
after me
until it splinters the tongue
  gas instead of petrol
  gas
  say it *gas*
not petrol
the operator can't understand
spell out your name again?
your name
when they recommend
you correct

CHORI MAAL

"We were not poor when we came...but this country tells us we are."

—Gurjinder Basran

chori maal
he sells
what "fell off the back
of the truck"
he sells
Chanel Bleu and
Gucci
we wear
what papa buys us from
Armando Benítez's perfume shop
each time
something stolen
something blue
wed to this way
of life
though we may live
distant
D.C. Atlanta Toronto
our undocumented life
  afraid to answer doorbells
we scent to pass

SHADE

partition slants the grass
slick
snaps the trees
white
gashes the roof
tongues
name the bigger light and how the less

'no dogs or indians'
shine my boots!
dadhaji in the sun
Viceroy in Phantom

all those stones
go home to your country
my country?
where we are on any map

did not celestial beings say
once we are born, throw us in the river—
in that way we shall be released
they knew something
of what it was to be
caught between worlds

no one notices
a redubber's dance

a Sikh girl chops hair for
two friends or three
like the Jennifers
a white man lusts

i never learned
how should i look?
this shade of wheat
i'm missing
between drought
to moon

i no longer wanted what shade did we begin?

carved over skin masks

WE BUILT NO GARDENS

we built no gardens

            simply turned

did you know a boy of 12
cuts his wrists
did you know what a girl
of nine must do for bread
in camps
            you know what the word
            future means when all things
limbs and blood
            scatter

go there there
            there
but not here!

it is us again
seeking place

"Leap over me if you must go
forward."
—The Mahabharata

"Here he is, large as life, by his
own fire, and you deny that he will
ever get home!"
—The Odyssey

COORDINATES

it's 4 a.m. and clear
   13 degrees centigrade
   in Jalalabad

   Google can't calculate the drive the
walk or how long it will take by TTC
   only shows the expanse of impossible
blue
   the mouth of the South Pacific
   the fingernail of Chile
   and Hawaii the crumbs

   i type:
"calculate distance between two coordinates"
and receive
the haversine formula

to calculate distance between two points—that is
the shortest distance over the earth's surface
and the bearing between two latitudes

purplemath.com promises
the distance formula its origin its use
the length of hypotenuse *is the distance between two*
points

   another
says to *just type your equations and let the calculator do*
the rest!
to find the distance between two points
(x1,y1) and (x2,y2)
all that you need to do is use the—

but all i want to know is
how far
from daughter
from mother
from herself she will be
from me
when she returns

MERIDIAN

scroll down
and see
the angular separation between Mizar and Alcor in Ursa
Major—
  see the spherical law of cosines
  about equirectangular approximation
  see that *accuracy is somewhat complex:*
along meridians there are no errors
    of bearing and midpoints
    of blue oceans yellow lines
red distances
our eyes can drink in as much of Baghdad to Osaka
        as we please
    great circular arcs will take us
places   even reverse
        between it all
        spaces transform

a language not my own   percentages
x's and y's
Δ's and λ's
i could never read

understand

if the blind can feel a smile
the weight of love in their fingers
then we should feel the tilt of the earth
fold into its axis
and know
it is not seeing
to arrive

beside me
scatter those i have yet to meet

scatter me
and you and you and you
each meter and mile
we arrive

RHUMB LINES

places where sailors cannot go

where people
shift their heavy loads

follow some great
constant compass

Pedro Nunes knew
that a steady path meant
one of spirals

and if you're in the mood for cantering through
such night-bruised winter
or navigating the stone-rocked Atlantic
it's helpful to know
such lines
          meridians
          lullabies

either way
we drift

BLANKS

maps feed distraction:
calculate distance between two cities
how far is it
from Tehran to Tel Aviv?

*

reminded of the many miles
we've traveled

(though we're no better or worse off)
often   just short of an exact distance
reminding us how far
from the soil we are
now

*

blogs read:
Washington's Uneasy Partnership With Tehran
or __________ (fill in the blank)

U.S. forces providing support to the Iranian troops
battling Sunni extremists in Iraq and Syria. Yemen could
be the next—

__________ providing support to the
__________ troops
battling __________ extremists
in __________ and __________
__________ could be the next

a game-card history

*

war breeds strange alliances

systematic shaping of geography and history by
civility and greed

cloth on medieval queens' corpses
tell of silk route outlaws

archeologists
near the village of Llanbedrgoch in north Wales
unearth fortified trading posts
uncover silver armbands with Viking marks
at a time when both sides were enemies

a blurred term   enemy

a price tag definition

what will we unearth
in other places

years from now
think of what will be said
of what's below ground

our drones our guns our __________

will it be as jarring as finding
the tusks of rusting tanks
shelled out ships in mountains
or the remains of a king in a parking lot?

TO WHAT PLACE

by ways of Hecabe, for my sister

in a country no longer hers
her chorus knew what things to say

to what place will you bring me?

but for those unpenned by Euripides
for those petrified into deep daily silences
for those who cannot claim to exist on any map

it is something else

*

i once sent my sister milk chocolates
wrapped in crinkling gold foil
12 ounces of French Vanilla coffee beans
caramels
a three-wick candle perfumed with
coconut
body lotions with casaba melon
freesia and plum
all to remind her

i am a goods peddler
distraction like Jasper Maskelyne
during the Second Great War
sending dummy props dummy gifts
dummy ruses

*

then i asked her
how she could sleep
knowing that at any time

  could she sleep right after
  doing what she

where are we all brought

there's nothing you can do but sleep in bulletproof vests
beneath the bed during
take the pills they give you to sleep

to what place has she been brought

a dust cloud to pass through on a tank
a place you stay without seeing the stars

*

before Jalalabad   and the compound
a fuggy bunker of 10 where the night insects
zither through the glasspaper walls   that you can't see
but you hear
when her FaceTime freezes
the womantalk

*

perhaps this is what Sun Tzu meant when he said
subdue the enemy without fighting

*

i didn't ask these questions of her   or of
anybody else
but now
to what place will we arrive

"...a constant and considerable stream of mental symptoms are direct sequels of this oppression."

—Frantz Fanon

PTSD SOUTH BEACH

freedombombs burst   inair
you taste
elsewhere
shudder sweat-stainedshirt
against concrete wall

hotel room where palm leaves
sway in east wind
or is it the room
the room that's swaying?

remember
kevlar and fear upon you
your D.C. daughter
your Pentagon husband
and perhaps
perhaps thosesandthats that you'd
never—

now   herewhere
they take it easy
motorcycles cumangry rage
engineoil over sandsprinkled
alwayssavageroads
where boys without juice in their balls   suck
cock
on South Beach
and tourists haggle over hats and beads

but you
you never left the base

here
is where we sit sister
facing a blistering ocean

here is where your skin sits too
your breath breathing
not therewhere
   somethingbleeding
still knuckles you tender   over
and over
tests you
over

screams
they stay the sounds

the way the ground quakes when it's still

CRAYONS

"an ancient palimpsest on which layer upon layer of thought and reverie had been inscribed, and yet no succeeding layer had completely hidden or erased what had been written previously."

—Jawaharlal Nehru

   my sisters and i
   on a mattress
   on the floor

   we didn't know
   box springs or duvets

of a world of order
white sheets
neat and crisp
tucked tight

we coloured on walls
broken crayons
from a Crayola box

nothing

everything

jagged scrawls

hungry beasts of dark planets
a language of "flesh" to "peach"
"Indian red" to "chestnut"
half formed caves
  open   shapes

unfunctionable for distinct interpretation

a loose unspeak

pounds of textbooks
"Trail of Tears"
over Pythagoras and
inflected verbs and protozoas
on our backs
urge us faster

we knew what colour bled us from a womb
we were in the midst of our own collisions
against skin
knowledge

the weight of names
where our parents were from
became *masala*
          okra on our shirts
folds of *roti* in foil
we smell
of turmeric and red dots
we do not read

our parents never abjured our folly
they watched these explosions   off paper
as shedding some earthly childhood

now
nieces and nephews
jazzberry jam
wild blue yonder
finger meteors   outside of orbits

discordant shades
mix with ease
joy colours disorder

i tell them undefinitions
embrace blurs everywhere
i try and tell them
colours
of the universe

REASONS TO THROW STONES

America begins
this way
48 Trenton St.
where i slowly ask
what i'd thought of for a year—
why did you leave me behind?

she sniffs and
immediately pulls me towards a bath alarmed
by the size of my long loose undergarments
stitched in India elastic frills and ribbons at
each end *you can't wear those!*
i'll have to take you
shopping!
sluicing me over the head with measuring
cups of soap

immediately America begins with a vigorous
scrubbing immediately i change and please so
immediately i know America is not for big
open questions my mother brandishes card
after card slashing through lines builds my
closet of each auditions next day *don't give*
them reasons to throw stones this she gives me
now i arrive in Canada i don't know what to
do immediately when i arrive to Canada what
to do immediately?

ACKNOWLEDGMENTS

I'd like to thank Denis De Klerck for believing in this book from the beginning. A special thanks to Jim Johnstone for his support in helping to edit this manuscript and Kristen Smith, who continues to inspire me.

And thanks finally to my husband, Gaurav Singh, for being my partner in life.

"alien alien" was previously published by *World Literature Today* (July 4, 2017).

"coordinates", "meridian", "rhumb lines", "blanks", "to what place" and "PTSD south beach" have previously appeared in the chapbook *PTSD south beach* (Grey Borders Books, 2016).

NOTES

Text in "alien alien" incorporates lines from Bon Jovi's song "Hey God".

Text in "shade" incorporates lines from the *Mahabharata: A Modern Retelling*. Translated by Carole Satyamurti, WW Norton, 2015.

Text in "coordinates" incorporates lines from two websites
Calculate distance, bearing and more between Latitude/Longitude points. Movable Type Scripts, http://www.movable-type.co.uk/scripts/latlong.html. Accessed 20 September 2017.
and
The Distance Formula. Math Warehouse,
http://www.mathwarehouse.com/algebra/distance_formula/index.php. Accessed 20 September 2017.

Text in "meridian" incorporates lines from the website
Calculate distance, bearing and more between Latitude/Longitude points. Movable Type Scripts, http://m.blog.csdn.net/yu412346928/article/de-

tails/42966297. Accessed 20 September 2017.

Text in “blanks” incorporates lines from “Washington’s Uneasy Partnership With Tehran Now Extends to Yemen.” Sean D. Naylor. *Foreign Policy*, 13 Feb. 2015. Web.

Text in “to what place” incorporates a line from Euripides’ *Hecabe*. Translated by Philip Vellacott, Penguin, 2002.

Puneet Dutt received her MA in English from Ryerson University. She is the author of the chapbook *PTSD south beach* (Grey Borders Books), which was a Finalist for the 2016 Breitling Chapbook Prize (Phantom Books). Her work has been published in a number of journals and in *Imaginarium 4: The Best Canadian Speculative Writing*. She was born in India and raised in New Jersey. She now resides in Toronto with her husband, where she is an editorial board member at *Canthius* and a creative writing workshop facilitator with the Toronto Writers Collective. She can be found online at *puneetdutt.com*.

Other Books From Mansfield Press

Poetry

Leanne Averbach, *Fever*
Tara Azzopardi, *Last Stop, Lonesome Town*
Nelson Ball, *In This Thin Rain*
Nelson Ball, *Some Mornings*
Nelson Ball, *Chewing Water*
Nelson Ball, *Walking*
Gary Barwin, *Moon Baboon Canoe*
Samantha Bernstein, *Spit on the Devil*
George Bowering, *Teeth: Poems 2006–2011*
Stephen Brockwell, *All of Us Reticent, Here, Together*
Stephen Brockwell, *Complete Surprising Fragments of Improbable Books*
Stephen Brockwell & Stuart Ross, eds., *Rogue Stimulus: The Stephen Harper Holiday Anthology for a Prorogued Parliament*
Diana Fitzgerald Bryden, *Learning Russian*
Alice Burdick, *Book of Short Sentences*
Alice Burdick, *Flutter*
Alice Burdick, *Holler*
Sarah Burgoyne, *Saint Twin*
Jason Camlot, *What The World Said*
Margaret Christakos, *wipe.under.a.love*
Pino Coluccio, *First Comes Love*
Marie-Ève Comtois, *My Planet of Kites*
Dani Couture, *YAW*
Gary Michael Dault, *The Milk of Birds*
Frank Davey, *Poems Suitable to Current Material Conditions*
Pier Giorgio Di Cicco, *The Dark Time of Angels*
Pier Giorgio Di Cicco, *Dead Men of the Fifties*
Pier Giorgio Di Cicco, *Early Works*
Pier Giorgio Di Cicco, *The Honeymoon Wilderness*
Pier Giorgio Di Cicco, *Living in Paradise*
Pier Giorgio Di Cicco, *My Life Without Me*
Pier Giorgio Di Cicco, *The Visible World*
Salvatore Difalco, *What Happens at Canals*
Christopher Doda, *Aesthetics Lesson*
Christopher Doda, *Among Ruins*
Christopher Doda, *Glutton for Punishment*
Glen Downie, *Monkey Soap*
Rishma Dunlop, *The Body of My Garden*
Rishma Dunlop, *Lover Through Departure: New and Selected Poems*
Rishma Dunlop, *Metropolis*
Rishma Dunlop & Priscila Uppal, eds., *Red Silk: An Anthology of South Asian Women Poets*
Ollivier Dyens, *The Profane Earth*
Laura Farina, *Some Talk of Being Human*
Jaime Forsythe, *Sympathy Loophole*
Carole Glasser Langille, *Late in a Slow Time*
Eva HD, *Rotten Perfect Mouth*
Eva HD, *Shiner*
Suzanne Hancock, *Another Name for Bridge*
Jason Heroux, *Emergency Hallelujah*
Jason Heroux, *Hard Work Cheering Up Sad Machines*
Jason Heroux, *Memoirs of an Alias*
Jason Heroux, *Natural Capital*
John B. Lee, *In the Terrible Weather of Guns*
Jeanette Lynes, *The Aging Cheerleader's Alphabet*
David W. McFadden, *Abnormal Brain Sonnets*
David W. McFadden, *Be Calm, Honey*
David W. McFadden, *Shouting Your Name Down the Well: Tankas and Haiku*
David W. McFadden, *What's the Score?*
Kathryn Mockler, *The Purpose Pitch*
Leigh Nash, *Goodbye, Ukulele*
Lillian Necakov, *The Bone Broker*
Lillian Necakov, *Hooligans*
Peter Norman, *At the Gates of the Theme Park*
Peter Norman, *Water Damage*
Natasha Nuhanovic, *Stray Dog Embassy*
Catherine Owen & Joe Rosenblatt, *Dog*
Corrado Paina, *The Alphabet of the Traveler*
Corrado Paina, *Cinematic Taxi*
Corrado Paina, *The Dowry of Education*
Corrado Paina, *Hoarse Legend*
Corrado Paina, *Souls in Plain Clothes*
Nick Papaxanthos, *Love Me Tender*
Branka Petrovic, *Mechanics of a Gaze*
Stuart Ross et al., *Our Days in Vaudeville*
Matt Santateresa, *A Beggar's Loom*
Matt Santateresa, *Icarus Redux*
Ann Shin, *The Last Thing Standing*
Jim Smith, *Back Off, Assassin! New and Selected Poems*
Jim Smith, *Happy Birthday, Nicanor Parra*
Robert Earl Stewart, *Campfire Radio Rhapsody*
Robert Earl Stewart, *Something Burned on the Southern Border*
Meaghan Strimas, *Yes Or Nope*
Carey Toane, *The Crystal Palace*
Aaron Tucker, *Punchlines*
Priscila Uppal, *Sabotage*
Priscila Uppal, *Summer Sport: Poems*
Priscila Uppal, *Winter Sport: Poems*
Steve Venright, *Floors of Enduring Beauty*
Brian Wickers, *Stations of the Lost*
Tara-Michelle Ziniuk, *Whatever, Iceberg*

Fiction

Marianne Apostolides, *The Lucky Child*
Sarah Dearing, *The Art of Sufficient Conclusions*
Denis De Klerck, ed., *Particle & Wave: A Mansfield Omnibus of Electro-Magnetic Fiction*
Salvatore Difalco, *Mean Season*
Paula Eisenstein, *Flip Turn*
Sara Heinonen, *Dear Leaves, I Miss You All*
Kascia Jaronczyk, *Lemons*
Christine Miscione, *Carafola*
Marko Sijan, *Mongrel*
Tom Walmsley, *Dog Eat Rat*
Corinne Wasilewski, *Live from the Underground*

Non-Fiction

George Bowering, *How I Wrote Certain of My Books*
Denis De Klerck & Corrado Paina, eds., *College Street–Little Italy: Toronto's Renaissance Strip*
Pier Giorgio Di Cicco, *Municipal Mind: Manifestos for the Creative City*
Amy Lavender Harris, *Imagining Toronto*
David W. McFadden, *Mother Died Last Summer*
Deborah Verginella, ed., *Buon Appetito Toronto!*

For a complete list of Mansfield Press titles, please visit mansfieldpress.net